PiLLAR OF BOOKS
책기둥

Pillar of Books

Moon Bo Young

Translated by Hedgie Choi

Black Ocean
Boston · Chicago

Black Ocean
P.O. Box 52030
Boston, MA 02205
blackocean.org

Cover Art and Design by Abby Haddican | abbyhaddican.com
Book Design by Taylor D. Waring |taylordwaring.com

ISBN: 978-1-939568-39-7

This book was published with the support of the Literature Translation Institute of Korea.

Library of Congress Control Number: 2021931839

FIRST EDITION

The gestation period of the confenurgen
is forty years —
the longest of any creature on Earth. But
the average lifespan of the confenurgen
is twenty-seven years —
what a riddle.

Winter, 2017
Moon Bo Young

CONTENTS

PART 3

PART 4

TRANSLATOR'S NOTE

On Tuesday June 1, 2018, I got a text from Jake Levine with a link to *Pillar of Books*. The text said "if you do poems by this lady/ that would be cool." At the time I was trying to figure out a polite way to tell Jake that I didn't want to translate anything ever again because translation is hard. It is like shoveling with your brain. I feel guilty saying this because I know there are people who think translation is an enriching and creative process. It enrages me that other people are able to find such joy and appreciation! I think translation is cool for a total of two seconds right after a poem first gets translated. Still, I said I'd take on translating *Pillar of Books* in part because I liked the poems a lot, in part because I was really bad at saying no to work. Now that I'm at the end of the process, was *Pillar of Books* an exception for me? Yes and no. It took over two years of hours and hours of brain shoveling: You take a comma out, you put a comma back in, you restructure a whole line so you don't have to use a comma, you restructure the whole poem so that the line is now broken, then you decide you liked it the first way better, so you revert to the original. You tell yourself you're never going to translate another syllable after this project. You swear you'll become monolingual. And that's how I feel after every project, but here I am at the end of *Pillar of Books* and I still really like Moon Bo Young's poems. That's kind of exceptional.

Here are some of the difficulties I had in translation:

Korean sentences have distinctive sentence-ending particles, and this makes punctuation far less important for comprehension compared to English. In the original, "Down Jacket God" has no periods. This has the effect of making the poem read flatly and quickly, almost like a run-on sentence, without sacrificing comprehension. Because the sentences are not separated by punctuation, "the poet writes" seems to ripple through all of these sentences, rather than merely the individual sentence. This was difficult to replicate in translation.

There is more flexibility with mixing tenses in Korean compared to English. For example, in "Lips" there is a mix of past and present tense, sometimes within stanzas or sentences. In the first draft of my translation, I replicated this exactly and found that the temporal relationships in English drew much more attention to themselves. They either looked like a mistake or forced some kind of narrative or causal relationship between events in the poem. In my revision, I unified the tense to present.

In Korean, conjunctions such as "but" and "and" are often appended as particles onto the last word of the clause rather than existing as a separate word. Because of this, they are used more casually and flexibly— they might be connecting what comes before with what comes after, but this isn't always the case. They might also be the end of a list or they might indicate trailing off. In "Lips," the last four stanzas end on such a conjunction. Sometimes that ambiguity has been carried over, but sometimes it got dropped because, once again, ambiguity can either seem like a mistake in English, or it forces a causal relationship that's not prominent in the original.

The most commonly used pronouns in this book are gender-neutral (Korean does have gender-specific pronouns, but they are generally less used and feel dated or romantic). In addition, while Korean does have plural pronouns, the singular pronoun can be used in place of the plural pronoun. Moon Bo Young's poems often use a singular gender-neutral pronoun to create ambiguity about who or how many people the pronoun is referring to. To maintain this intentional ambiguity, I used the "they" pronoun throughout the translation of the book.

And here are some of the joys:

Moon Bo Young is both super-funny and super-serious. "Down Jacket God" is a good example of this—it's also the first poem in her book. There's levity and surrealism, but there's also God and Death. The poet exists explicitly in this poem, breaking the fourth wall and writing in real time, but it seems like an exaggeration to say that this ironic move "undercuts" the rest of the poem. Rather than undercutting, there's juxtaposition and playful interaction. These elements are all there, together—God and Death and Love and Literature hanging out with feathers, chopsticks, a blanket being dusted, and little bugs—and the poet is tinkering with all of them, without reverence but with great curiosity.

Yeah.

Hm... what exactly is a translator's note for? What else can I say here?

Oh, I've been in correspondence with Moon Bo Young on and off, mostly to get her to sign contracts and permission notes so I can get these translations into literary magazines. She seems nice—I mean, it'd be whack if she managed to be rude in the tiny capacity of professional exchange we've had so far, but sometimes people really surprise you in the worst ways. She said she wanted to buy me dinner when I came back to Korea! (I know she loves pizza, but I hope she's open to shabu shabu.) We're friends on Facebook. If I had an Instagram, we would be Instagram friends. Is that a thing on Instagram? She has a cool Instagram, I think. I don't know, I haven't really looked at anyone else's Instagram. But from her Instagram, it looks like she modelled for Nike recently, and also, she dances? That enrages me too, that she's a great writer and also has many other talents. It's weird to translate someone who's alive and your age and way cooler than you.

PART I

DOWN JACKET GOD

God wears a massive down jacket. Humans are the countless duck feathers trapped inside, the poet writes. Sometimes a feather pokes out. God plucks it carelessly. That's what people call death. A feather gets plucked. That person dies. A feather gets plucked. That person expires. A feather gets plucked. That person breathes their last breath. A feather gets plucked. That person disappears.

After death there's no heaven or hell, no angels or devils, the poet writes. There's only a feather. It swings in the air. Gently, the feather settles on the ground.

ENTRANCE BLASPHEMY

Instead of wages, God ordered his minions to give those who entered the world Costco bread. People were born. Those of us who didn't get bread were baffled. We gathered for a deep think. *Why didn't we get bread?*

1)   We had only one outfit. Wearing undershirts with stretched-out necks, we joined the world pantless.
2)   Wishing for a soul shaped like an English pipe, we blasphemed.
3)   We thought that the woman who sat on the pews of the Catholic church looked like a scab growing over a wound.
4)   All our dreams were exciting. We wanted to swap reality for dreams.
5)   We watched God and wondered, *Does God have a digestive issue?*
6)   A *solid person*, what does that even mean?
7)   We didn't go to school much.
9)   We hoped we wouldn't want to be the kind of people who wanted to save books if the libraries of the world burned.
10) We read too many books.
11) So we became afraid of hope.
12) So a crazy dog kept chasing us.
13) So we kept running, running, running.

We're waiting for bread.

" _____ *"

1

In Kafka's *The Trial* there's actually a sentence that goes "_____ *" The only person who's seen that sentence is me. I looked in the back of the book for what the asterisk refers to, but there was no explanation. So is "_____*" Kafka's sentence? Or is Kafka citing a friend? Or is Kafka quoting me? The sentence "_____*" only exists in my eyes. Who besides me can help Kafka?

2

In Kafka's childhood in my head
I found the answer to "_____*"
When Kafka was a child
he thought people on the phone couldn't see.
When Kafka's mom was on the phone
she didn't scold little Kafka
who climbed on top of the refrigerator
and sat like a cobra.
She didn't even pay attention to him.
It was as if she thought he wasn't a person.
This was because a person
can only perceive one space
at a time. That's the beginning
of all suffering.

3

The cobra on the refrigerator looks down at a faraway branch.

4

"_____*" is repeated later in Kafka's life.

When Kafka complained, *I couldn't sleep*, Kafka's lover replied, *No*. When Kafka claimed, *Someone is trying to kill me*, those who were not Kafka replied in chorus, *No*. When Kafka opined that *Today is either spring, summer, fall, or winter*, all the readers of the future said, *No*.

5

Finally, the account of how Kafka wrote "   *" is as
    follows.   _____

6

I'm sitting on a refrigerator in Kafka's head.
When something scary
like a quiet Kafka appears beneath my feet
I repeat the following sentence:
If Earth looks like a period from far away, quick—
write the next sentence.
The cobra that lives on top of the refrigerator is silent.
The cobra is blind.

WALL

Everything that suffers from walls becomes a house. Everything addicted to walls becomes a wall. Just as everything that's born a wall and lives as a wall dies a wall, walls repeat and walls appear at random. "Though flowers bloom, I've never forgotten you." Should this sentence be read to scare? To comfort? Walls like fallen cedar trees and unanswered letters. No, the things that are like fallen cedar trees and unanswered letters are a wall. When you drill through a wall another wall appears. What are some other ways walls and sentence endings differ? Spring means spring even after it turns over a new leaf, and all faraway things are walls. A wall dedicates its life to vindicating other walls, but still. There's nothing written on the wall, and. No, things with nothing written on them are walls. The wall has no intention, and. The wall wants to be reckless, and. The wall's always in a critical state. As much as you believe it can hurt, the wall hurts. As much as you believe it can break, the wall crumbles. Walls are over-the-top or walls are inadequate. When a wall told the truth about the wall, where did the wall go? Even the wall that shed its wall became a wall.

INSOMNIA

Lying down, I look at my face profile.
2AM lays next to me. It wraps itself up in the gray throw and
    falls asleep before I do.

If my feet that poke a bit outside the blanket
were somebody else's feet, that'd be cool.

My lover is real healthy
even in the face of my death, but

I lean on my face profile and try to sleep.
Using my face profile as a pillow, I sleep.
Even in my dream I catch a cold.
The cold lasts several years
but I'm still standing on the floors of my feet.
Bearing down firmly on the floors of my feet
I bend over the ground like a street lamp.

Morning brightens tenaciously
even if you hide inside a blanket.

My face profile inhales other face profiles
like butane, and still

someone dies
neatly, like an apple.
Well-peeled.

WHAT GOT SEEN BY THE TWO EARS A PASSING DOG ATE

In the middle of the street. Z's beloved S said something awful to Z and Z's ears fell to the ground. A passing dog didn't hesitate to scarf them down. Z's two ears died before Z. They arrived in heaven before Z. But the ears were still in the dog's stomach, so Z had to listen to the sounds in the dog's stomach for the rest of Z's life.

Who's your father?
It's too small.
Where do you live, exactly?
I said, can you pass the sugar?

These strangers' words
sounded like they came from inside the dog's stomach.

The following are sounds from inside the dog's stomach translated
    into human language.

*

The dead ears went to heaven and had a look around.

1. Angels

Like bunching eraser dust into gray balls, angels recycle dead people's
   hearts by rolling them in circles.

2. Telescope

The newly independent ears
try closing and opening their eyes.
They can see.
Angels are stacked like
a heap of fish
in the corner of an old room.
They sleep with their faces left on
like TVs.
God appears
out of nowhere
and turns off their faces.
At the window is an old telescope with its bowed head.
The ears observe Earth through the telescope.
Earth is the shape
of a coin return slot
on a vending machine
placed alone in the corner
of a dark library.

3. Education

Even in heaven 44.5° C is fatal for wasps. Even in heaven they teach
   you Survival 101. The ears take notes.
Surrounded by 500 honeybees that violently shake their bellies and
   emanate a terrible heat, a single hornet has almost no hope of
   making it out. Not even in heaven.
Even in heaven
someone is panting and saying ridiculous shit like *Yeah, I'm on
   my way*, as they strut through the midday street.

4. Heaven

Can you be suspended indefinitely
even in heaven?

A leaf flutters by.

Z's ears
wait patiently
for Z to be as dead
as Z's ears are.
All Z's other parts will die someday too.
Somewhere
things get worn down.

5. Spoon

As in life, Z's father is an atheist after death. But his wife still prays
  before every meal.

> *Have you . . . anything to say to God . . . ?*

At the table the husband chucks his spoon up in the air.

> *You quack!*

the man shouts at God.

Because opposing forces exist everywhere, *squeak, squeak,* the world
  turns.

6. Happiness

Someone is happy.
Just to balance it out
someone gets sad.

7. God

The two cut off ears lie back and think
God is
a lazy, crafty

unmoved mover who
forces everyone to move while not moving a finger himself.
No, that won't do.
Woken by the sound of rain
kicking blankets
and dashing out
to bring in the laundry hanging on the rooftop
God
runs toward the world and gathers wet laundry.
God snatches the laundry off the line, but descending the stairs
God drops an undershirt.
This is God's one sin.

*

It was midday when the dog who swallowed a pair of ears walked by.
Could you tell us your current address?
There too, wind
as stupid as this question blew.

If you want to say
I'm a slightly dead person
it doesn't matter who you are.
You must have a partly visible wound.

HAT

Put on the hat and it comes. Take off the hat and it disappears. A thought starts with the hat. When the hat ends, the thought becomes deficient. Take off the hat and become curious. Put on the hat and want to forget. There's a big land inside the hat. A cow herd rumbles across it. I want to take off my thoughts. Put on the hat and thought sets up camp on top of the head. Someone sees the hat and exaggerates, *That person walks around with a dead house on their head.* The sentence *This isn't a dead house, this is a dead thought* is half-baked. Take off the hat and the sentence turns in its tracks. The hat makes it stop. Wearing the hat isn't the same as overcoming the hat. Thoughts that failed the hat cry. They cry so hard we need a contrasting image. The hat is brought up again. The hat has never cried. When it was born, a hiccup then silence. Someone sees the hat and shouts, *That person walks around with a big land on their head!* That person doesn't see the big dust cloud of the big cow herd on the big land. I put on the hat. It appears: The big, dark land. The world the hat knows. The sadness of the hat can't grow because it has a band around it. The hat can't understand that. The hat is sad with no understanding. The thought that the hat's sadness is the same as wooden chopsticks that can't be split apart is half-baked. I bring up the hat. I stop the hat. I believe I understand the hat as much as I wear it. *If you were more dedicated, it would become sadness,* says the hat, believes the hat. I put on the hat. The hat covers my head the way a scab grows over a wound. *Wearing the hat doesn't cause new skin to grow, and I have no intention of reading into it that much,* warns the hat, forgets the hat. *If you saw the dead cow herd that fell off a cliff after running indiscriminately all over the big land, you would know,* says the hat. But the hat doesn't live by this statement. *Do you know me?* screams the hat. The hat leans toward my left shoulder. A bit. I'm pretty sure I understand the hat. A bit.

TWO COLORS IN A PICTURE BOOK

This picture book is horizontal and composed of only two colors. Color 1 and Color 2 are equally unimportant. That by itself intrigues the reader.

If a character dies on the left page, the right page rejects it. Because only two colors exist in the picture book, coloring shadows isn't a real possibility.

The fact that someone has died disrupts the narrative flow. It's a kind of manpower shortage. It reflects the writer's inability to save people. Also, being unwilling to keep people alive is the writer's trademark.

Let's not ignore the fact that in order to illustrate one death, at least two people are spared.

Could the slight gap under the barn's roof represent the death of the character inside? The author has only two colors. The author's material impoverishment is so typical. But doesn't that only glorify this irresponsible death?

Saving a person from death and not saving a person from death appear to be equally important. This betrays the reader's curiosity.

Two colors are enough to express death's spatial depth. *Quit it. The way you're going, you're going to wreck someone.* One or two lines of dialogue per page is enough for a picture book.

The right page and left page can't agree on how to allude to the corpse's back. So death is delayed. In the end each page sticks to its own method. In the end the reader believes two people die. *That's a trademark of the writer,* says the children's book critic who wears his hat backwards.

The reader's interpretation
that the corpses are depicted like that
because there wasn't enough money for the artist to buy paint *is* a
    fantasy, and
the praise people give
because they think that great work was created serendipitously through
    the writer's poverty
is equally unimportant.
That by itself intrigues the reader.

Turning the page is like opening the lid to a coffin.
Every time the coffin opens
the perspective of the world
of the person inside
gets changed.

COLLABORATION POEM

The young poets Antoine, Gemelle, and Strains atten a poetry lecture.
    The sun flaps white like a t-shirt on a clothesline.

The poet at the podium scatters different sized bananas on the floor.
The readers each take a banana.
The banana between bananas vanishes
and a banana moves
and a banana disappears.
This is how art forms change,
says the poet at the podium.
The readers and the poet go bananas and
they become banana-rich.

Gemelle, Antoine, and Strains are jealous.

I want to do it too!

They shout internally. Each return to their separate houses to work on
    a collaboration.

*

Gemelle cloisters herself in her room. She writes a poem about the
    reader and a crab.
A long-necked reader walks down the trail.
A crab appears and blocks the path.

She goes this way
and the crab crab-walks and blocks her.
She goes that way
and the crab crab-walks and blocks her.
The poet crab-walks
to interrupt the reader.

*

Antoine
writes about a poem-writing scorpion.
The scorpion grabs the hard-to-grab pencil
with its stumpy claws
and writes a poem.

In the dream
is a self
that wants to be spilt
out of the dream

. . .

The reader glances over. The scorpion
takes the pencil and stabs the reader's eyes.

Like two perfect circles
drawn by a compass,
me in the dream

and me outside the dream
are enemies.
Tossing and turning . . .

Chills go down the scorpion's spine.

The reader returns with new eyeballs
and glances at the scorpion's poem.

Don't look!
I said don't look! The scorpion stabs
the reader's eyes.
The scorpion picks up the stubby pencil from the ground.

No one stops me from waking up from the dream . . .

When the reader returns
the scorpion stabs the reader's eyeballs.
Splork!
Like popping a fish's swim bladder, an air pocket
bursts. Stab and
write, stab and write, stab
and write.
Eyeball liquid
soggies stylistics.

*

Strains writes a poem with a walking stick. Whipping the walking
    stick, Strains thinks no thought.
A thought comes to Strains.

It's an escalator.
The poet on a very long escalator
is surprised. A reader is ahead.
A reader, even here! The walking stick
freaks out.

Someone fiddles with their hair. The reader stands behind someone and
covers balding spots with hair. Against their will, the poet's arms cover
the baldness of someone in front of them. Everyone on the escalator is
balding. Someone in front covers the baldness of someone in front of
someone, and that someone covers the baldness of someone in front
of someone in front of someone ahead, and that someone covers the
baldness of someone in front of someone in front of someone in front
of someone in front with what barely-there hair is left. The escalator
operates with the force of something barely-there covering a barely-there
thing, and so

even in the poem the poet can drop the walking stick.

*

The young poets Gemelle, Antoine, and Strains have fun with the
    reader in their separate houses. Lying in some alley in town is a
    corpse, swarming with gnats, annoyed by death.

The sun is bright.
The corpse's heart rots on. No one is touched.

SELF-DEFENSE

Person A
doesn't read.
Person A is afraid there will be no more books in the world to read
if they read all the books.

*

The library helps out Person A.

*

Book [ ] part 2, part 3, part 4...
Book [ ] part 2, part 3, part 4...
Book [ ] part 2, part 3, part 4...
Book [ ] part 2, part 3, part 4...
Book [ ] part 2, part 3, part 4...

*

Every library book begins at chapter 2.
All great books have no beginning,
thinks Person A.

*

The library binds all the first chapters in chains
and hides them in the basement.
Dogs and wind guard the entrance.

*

The library protects itself from people and

*

the library fills and bulks up on books.
The library begins to breathe
like a person.

PART 2

BIG-FACED PERSON

A photo studio.
A group photo.
Six people.

Person A never got married, but is thrice divorced.
There's a crater tattooed on the back of Person B's neck.
Person C is actually a good person once you get to know them.
Person D is easily intimidated by umbrella spokes.
Person E's face is the same whether or not they hold their breath.
Person F doesn't wear a bra.

To look nice in the photo
Person A has been exercising
Person B got her beauty sleep
Person C and D hug and
Person E recalls positive experiences.

F should make an effort too, but
she has no bra. She's wearing a loose
white cotton T-shirt so
her nipples flash when she straightens her back.
She slouches on a chair
with her head bowed.
Effort is impossible without a bra.

Person A, Person B, Person C, Person D, and Person E approach F.
Why are you slouching?
Can't you straighten your back?
Can we help?

F can't lift her head because she doesn't have a bra.
With her head bowed, she looks sideways at everyone else's breasts.

All perfectly concealed!

Where are the bras? The more
she thinks about it the more it seems
that bras are allowed for everyone
except F.

Slouched F sticks out her neck.
The photographer presses the shutter.

In the photo
out of A, B, C, D, E, and F
F has the biggest face.

BRAIN AND ME

My lover forgot their brain when they left. I could blend it and drink it, I guess. I examine and feel this human brain. I put a blonde wig on it, close its eyes, dunk it in warm water. I give it a poke.

The brain feels no pain. While receiving open-head surgery a patient could listen to *Beethoven's Symphony No. 9* or *Rachmaninoff's Prelude Op 23 No. 5*. The patient could discuss the level of blood loss or the likelihood of failure with the surgeon. The brain allows for very human activities.

The brain relaxes on a leather couch in the living room. It's the first time the brain has sat on something soft. The brain looks out the window with its cauliflower face.

*

The brain tends to loop its last memory.

The amusement park carousel spins.
People wave to a girl.
The girl waves from outside the fence.
Even to the girl staring at her.
They're all holding a weird thing.
Cylindrical clear sticks
with hands attached to the ends.

Toys.
Cylinders filled with rainbow gobstoppers.
People with hands
go out of their way to buy more hands and
wave them. The girl also
waves her hand at the girl waving her hand.
The girl thinks about the pointless wrinkle
that appears on the girl's forehead
when the girl's bangs are swept in the wind.
Is it really true that the brain feels no pain?

*

The brain has one defect. It remembers more than it sees. A considerable amount of DNA gets damaged as a result. What mechanism does the brain use to make memories? This is a very difficult question, but since the etymology of the word for the brain's nerve cell, neuron, comes from rope, we can guess that a rope is used.

*

The brain is still sitting on the sofa. I open the window and the wind cools off the brain. Miyashita Yasushi sticks electrodes on monkeys' brains and observes the reactions of their temporal lobes. It rains outside the window. Someone hangs outside the window. The window has a tendency to exaggerate smiles. Miyashita Yasushi plugs electrodes to the monkey's brain.

(He shows the monkey a circle, a square, a star.)

The monkeys' reaction: no reaction.

(He shows the monkey a person.)

The monkeys' reaction: a small reaction, then nothing.

(He shows the monkey a monkey.)

The monkeys' reaction: sustained reaction.

Miyashita studies the attention disparity. Why do monkeys only pay sustained attention to other monkeys? Some people might be saddened by this fact. Why does the hanging person outside the window grin on a rainy day? How did he get to the 21st floor without a rope? Since the word neuron comes from rope, when you have a memory you want to forget, just tie it up.

*

I'm laying thoughts to sleep
like spraying down the lawn with water
during a hot summer.
The flat cloud that can't cover the sky
covers the person who covers
their ears with hair.

Someone hangs from the window.
I pinch the end of the hose to increase the pressure.
Flowers beaten by
blue blue water.
Someone hangs from the window without a rope.

I hold my pencil upside down
and smush the little eraser
into the brain's side. The brain
won't break and
underneath a tree that fell asleep without hugging anything
the soft spores the brain blows look like the milky way and
the brain sleeps like an old mushroom head.
Soft, but hard.
When I poke the brain
its body shrivels.
Blood pools black-red between wrinkles.
When I lift the pressure
the brain swells.
The blood pooled between wrinkles is reabsorbed.

*

When I chew a biscuit
the chewing sounds loud to me
but you can barely hear it.

Let's use the rope.
I'll throw the rope and you tie it to your wrist.
Then my chewing will sound loud to you too.
Tie a rope to the handles
of two doors that face each other.
Let the wind in. Out.

*

Sticky green strings with sections cut,
neurons spill to the floor.
It's like you spilled an almost empty tub of green paint.
Kleist tightly grips his pencil to map the cerebral cortex's functions.
He gets out an electron microscope.
The desire to see what's hard to see by zooming in 5 billion times springs
from an evil mind.

Changing the way neurons are connected creates a memory,
    another old rope
about-to-snap.

*

I put on rubber gloves and
raise the brain with both hands.
I observe the wide and flabby brain.

I don't have to chew it to know it's tough.
The brain doesn't rub its eye or drool.
It doesn't get cold sweats.
You can't lock eyes with the brain.
Any way you look
you only see the brain from its side.
When it gets stressed blood pools in the wrinkles of the brain.
The wrinkles are thick and clearly defined.

*

This is the story of someone hanging from the window alone.

LIPS

I inspect the half pair of lips. I put them down. I can't read the lips.
    We become lovers.

Your lips taste like the damp floor of a seafood factory
or a worker's wet, plastic apron.

Children in the alley swarm.
When they cry, they cry together like a flock.
That's what your lips sound like.
I bite those lips hard and
the soles of your feet darken with desperation.

As inevitably as tomorrow arrives
lips move over lips.

Someone went up to their balcony to dust off a blanket and fell
and died and some person
surged up from the soles of their shoes.
They climbed over the lips and fell.
That's how dead people look.
Lips are like corpse's feet that have been carelessly arranged.
They have no direction and

if you stay silent for long, you will feel like your lips have vanished.
Like unseparated chopsticks, maybe the lips went missing, so
dozens of times a day you check to see if they're still there
growing suspicious
right beneath your nose.

FALLEN KID

I want to drink water and

there's this fallen kid.

I want to drink water but

there's this fallen kid.

Because I need to drink water

some kid fell and I

need to eat this kid, but

the water fell.

Depending on the circumstances

I'm either water or the fallen kid, but

even if we fall, the kid pledges not to fall like water, and

falls like water.

There's a kid here.

HISTORY AND THE HAND OF GOD

1

The man is reading Mochizuki Ryoko's *Hand of God*. He lays down his briefcase flat-side-down on the green rubber desk and angles *Hand of God* on top of it. He adjusts the angle so that he can see the *Hand of God*. He's suddenly sleepy. There's another pair of eyes staring at him. It's the big-eyed woman sitting at another desk, reading a history book.

The curtains come down on the war. The history book the woman is
    reading repeats the same line.
       decision-consequence
       decision-consequence
       decision-consequence
It's a history book but
it contains only history and war.
The history book can say, as it did just now
what history doesn't say:
The world ended and the only thing left is stain removal.
The world ended but people don't stop craving powerful
    ingredients
so every book title became *Hand of God* and everyone headed to the
library.

The man reading
the book about history and war and stain removal
dozed off and
even though it wasn't because he dozed
the *Hand of God* slipped away from him. He
was sure he was holding the *Hand of God* with both hands, but
people who hold the *Hand of God* with both hands get tired
    quicker than others.

2

It's always
1PM or 3PM
in the library and
like 1PM or 3PM
the library is insincere.

3

Because only people who
don't exist like
national holidays
flow into
the library.

4

There are always two people you know in the world.
Angela Rosa and Rosa.
Because you knew Angela Rosa before you knew Rosa
when you call Rosa's name
you must first think of Angela Rosa and then remove the Angela.
Rosa always seems longer, fussier, and more stain-ridden than
    Angela Rosa to you.

5

The people who look for Rosa only look for her in books.
There's no Rosa in reality. She exists only in history.
You count how many "decision-consequence" pairs there are in this
    book.
That number is the same as the number of characters killed
and so counting the number of "decision-consequence" pairs helps
    you
at the supermarket when you're trying to calculate
how many tubs of stain remover you should put in your cart.

6

People read books.
Someone on vacation calls someone else on vacation

7

countlessly.

8

The man
who the *Hand of God* slipped away from
put the *Hand of God* facedown on top of his backpack
so that anyone could glimpse
at God cupping God's face with God's two hands.
Thinking that it's possible
to begin reading where he left off
when he gets back
the man gets up.
He reaches inside the backpack pocket
with the broken zipper
that can't be closed,
the left one, and
pulls out a bag of star-shaped cheese snacks.
The man leaves
the library.

ROAD

My eyes open every day, and I nightmare
diligently.

I stick a cypress in an empty alley, and
the alley becomes closed-minded.

I try opening my eyes because I'm narrow.

I want to sprint
to shed my back.

If I run an open road
I'll have the feeling of truing my whole body.
If I open my eyes wide, I'll see my back instead of what's in front of me.

As if my back is my abnormality.

The more I run the stronger my back gets
so I keep my eyes open wide

because keeping your eyes open wide
means you won't make eye contact with anything.

The faster I run the more my back catches up with me and

when I stop
my back falls first.
I vanish.

The point outside the triangle is a white elephant

born from negligence.

Person *a* throws trash out the window.

He throws as far as he can

but the trash comes back.

The point outside the triangle is hungry.

Can a point have an empty stomach?

The point is non-intelligent, so how is it screaming?

Person a threw the smelly trash out the window

making an inside thing outside.

The point outside the triangle hurts.

An accidental point ticked outside the triangle.

The innocent point asks dumb questions.

Why is the person that ticked me watching me so closely?

Why is the surprisingly dismal point conscious of this space?

POSSIBLE SUMMER FOR A FLY

Uncertain Snake is a movie about three characters
who jump around every time the snake pops out.
One person jumps. Someone else hops out of the darkness.
Someone else hops out of a different darkness.
They bend and extend their knees, hop
hop hop hopping,
surprised, surprised
again and again by the snake.

The young poets Antoine, Gemelle, and Strains watch *Uncertain Snake*
    and head home.
Summer, mid-day
a wad of gum that sticks to the floor is stuck there forever.

Antoine: What will you do when you get home?
Gemelle: I think I'll eat some ice cream and scribble in my
    brainstorming book.
Antoine: (falling over backwards) You have a brainstorming book?
    How cheesy!
Strains: (swinging a staff) I have a brainstorming book too! It's for
    writing down useless things.

One fly sits
on the wide brim of Antoine's hat
that has a parrot feather
poked into it simply and honestly.

It's summer.
It's hard to endure even if you don't move.

Silence. The three of them think of their brainstorming books.
    The books are really useless so they keep their mouths shut.
    Filthy pigeons walk around on the road. A short man with
    headphones
around his neck wants to check
if he can see himself inside a pigeon's eye
so he runs toward a pigeon and

the pigeon pretends to be alarmed and sidesteps him. It's
summer.
The fly is in another context.
Even in that other context, the fly stays still.

Strains: (shaking the fanny pack around her waist) You guys
    want an ice cream?

Strains smiles, showing her innocent teeth. The fly
takes its thin feet off the brim of Antoine's hat
and slowly flies around the three poets. The sentence
A virtue of the fly is that it doesn't try to express its thoughts
could be written in a brainstorming book.
It's that kind of summer.

Antoine: Can I show you my brainstorming book?
Gemelle and Strains: (simultaneously) No!
Gemelle: Can I show you mine?
Antoine and Strains: (plugging their ears) No!
Strains: You want to see mine?
Antoine and Gemelle: (clapping their hands on Strains' mouth) No!

The fly buzzes. Antoine, Gemelle and Strains think *Fly* . . . but Strains is the one who thinks *Fly* . . . the most, so she takes the staff she dropped when she plugged her ears and swings it at the fly. The fly flies slowly in the heat. Because the staff's swinging is faster than the fly's flying, the fly gets whisked, not to death, just away. It's that kind of summer.

Someone might put
The season of needless fly swatting
into their brainstorming book. Actually

the movie *Uncertain Snake* has a protagonist
but the protagonist dies before the snake shows.
The protagonist dies so fast no one knows they're the protagonist.
It's always like that. *It's such a sad movie*
thought nobody, and so
it's summer,
that season when not being sad is a part of being sad.
The fly hangs around the three poets again.
It's always like that.
Whether the fly is well or poor, it always hovers around someone.

Hovering around, getting smacked and not dying,
those are virtues of the fly.

In the corner of a poem in the brainstorming book in which a fly
     appears
the poet scribbles down
Conditions necessary for a fly to live humanely
and closes the book. The poet thinks
Writing poems is such a useful human game.
It's possible to think this
because it's that kind of summer.

WHY IS JAYWALKING NECESSARY?

She was born too early.
Because God jaywalked

were the first lines of a poem that Dominic wrote.
Then he erased the following stanzas.

The small shit beneath the utility pole was calm on the outside, but it was such a scared shit that it was more afraid of the raining midday than the pitch-black night. It tried to be vigilant. When it was night it kept its mouth shut, even though it realized something was going very wrong.

She was born too early. The book named Barcena who gave birth to Dominic. She realized early on that anywhere you can't be sad is a mental hospital. Because she went to school early, she was kicked out early, and lived the life of a tasty round grape under a press, not squished yet, trying to be just fine. Because she knew love early, she thought often of the little shit, and if a slight erasure is allowed for humans—though it will hurt God's pride in his profession—she wanted to be the shit under the utility pole, no, she wanted to be the shit's calmness itself, and she didn't know what was going on inside this shit who was more afraid of the raining midday than the pitch-black night but if she had known its inner life she really would've been in deep shit. The giant mole that covered her left nostril was so big that her skin would have to be carved away in order to erase it and then she would have to live noseless, which she thought wasn't a bad option, but the wide mole kept its station on her face until she died. The plump brown mole that covered the left side of her nose turned everyone against her. This allowed her to maintain a consistent attitude toward life until death. On the day God jaywalked, God jaywalked because God didn't want to die. This God felt genuinely. At this point we can quote a line from this poem's author, Barcena's son Dominic, *it's true that humans are less humane than God.* When Dominic was sliding down the canal that fetuses come out of, he saw a man rushing across a street, undoing the countless buttons lining his coat as if he was trying to take off his body, and a single round button was about to fall, or wanting to fall, no, the button had fallen off several times in the past and had been reattached but was dangling again, ready to come off, and baby Dominic saw that small button was the world he was going to be born into, and even knowing this, baby Dominic was calm. Let's return to Barcena's life. She left the world early, early. This last sentence sufficiently illustrates her stance towards loose buttons that have fallen off.

LAWS OF SCIENCE

1

A slept with B and C and D and E and F and G and H. Always at the moment of climax a quote from Democritus rang in A's head. *Everything is a random combination of atoms!* Though A slept with I and J and K and L and M, Democritus wouldn't take back what he said. Everything is a random combination of atoms, nothing has essence.

2

Poems seek explanations for observed phenomena that rely solely on
   natural rather than supernatural causes.
Poems progress through the creation and testing of models of nature
   that explain the observations as simply as possible.
Poems must make testable predictions about natural phenomena that
   would force us to revise or abandon the model if the predictions
   don't agree with observations.

3

The laws of gravity don't apply to the world of particles smaller than atoms. This is because God is a microorganism smaller than the atom. It's not that we can't see God because God is too big; it's that God is too small to be seen with the naked eye. We need special equipment to see God. To cut off contact with humans, God stopped the laws of gravity in the human world from affecting God's world and now the humans are hurt.

4

a is *a* to the power of 1 but it pretends not to be. Here, 1 is something like air. There's no need to announce that it's there. People were lonely so they pinky promised that the power of 1 can be omitted unlike squares or cubes. Not writing 1 is a kind of strategy, and/or mental training.

5

There is an invisible steep slope in the sky, so the birds keep slipping.

6

Two high school girls sit at the back of the bus.
Eunseong, what time is it?
It's 4:24.

Person *a* is hurt.
They didn't want to know what time it is in this world; they
    didn't want to hear anything so scary...

Person *a* thinks

The Earth's radius is approximately 6400km, so
use the equation 2 π r to determine the circumference and divide that
    by 24 hours: the Earth is running at 1674km per hour.
Therefore
Person *a* has to be running the opposite direction of the Earth at
    1674km per hour
in order to look calm and still, in order for the universe to look calm
    and still, from the point of view of the universe.
Person a was running, running, running to forget the world so
why were people talking about what time it was?

7

You scratch your head. If you have a period five times in a month,
    your nails have specks of dried blood stuck under them.

REDSTREAMMONKEY

A monkey's butt runs
Trains are red
Trees run and
refrigerators are standing
Windows
store a rotten ham on the top shelf
Children's books keep passing by
Shutter, for adults
The rain drags down
The house can't
The coward shuts the door
Life is too much
A knee isn't a house
The worm stretches
A liverless sentence wants to hug a sentence
with a liver
The rain has lost it
Trees drip down
The ruler can't speak precisely
and misfortune measures
You can't repress a window
The stamp keeps passing
Next to
the red monkey
Red pebble's gentle smiles poking their faces out from under the red
    stream

SPARE PARTS

The writer, who sits at their wooden desk and preys on cherry
    tomatoes, goes into the forest for firewood. It's fodder for
    the man in the book.

In the book there is a wet wood table, wood chair, and wood
    bed. The wanderer on the bed who doesn't fit the bed
    looks at the wood framed window. The wanderer's first
    impression is that the window won't open.

Arms and legs that were chopped off for causing chaos in the
    mind.
Blood that runs everywhere, directionless.
It can't rain in the story but the man in the story
stands barefoot on the wet floor and says
I wish rain, or whatever it is, would let up.

In the forest the writer cloaked with leaves waits
for wanderers with long limbs.
Only wanderers who are somehow too much or lacking in some way
    are useful.
That's the shared opinion of clumsy writers.
A wanderer with needlessly long limbs passes by.
The writer attacks from behind and throws them
into the book.

Hungry,
the shadow's image sinks its teeth into a tree.
The man in the book who has been staring at the shadow
lays the wanderer down on the bed and sharpens his saw. Pumpkin-
yellow,
the wanderer's scared face.
Based on my experience, this is a dream. This awareness does little to
    reduce the terror.

The wanderer looks at the window. The impression that the
    window won't open is a terror someone else has used already,
    so the wanderer
adds to the impression of the window
with this terror: *Even if that window opened, what's outside it isn't real.*

The writer kidnaps a wanderer who doesn't fit on the bed, throws
    the wanderer to the man in the book, and washes their hands,
    careless as someone who shakes a near-empty bottle of gas a
    couple times and lights it with a flick. That is
contrary to what a certain reader thinks:
*Doesn't every story come from some scheme that's been thought through
    piece by piece?*

The readers reap deep knowledge about the limbs that were cut away.
The writer preys on cherry tomatoes and falls into complacent
    thoughts.
The wanderer is laid out on the bed:

Based on my experience, this isn't a dream. This awareness does nothing
     to enhance quick-thinking.

Dark and gloomy room.
Wet floors and the fishy tang of blood.
The man in the book
opens the window a little for ventilation. A little light seeps outside.
The seeped-out light
was always reality.

WHITE FACTORY

The research center is a cube building with a neat chimney plunged into the right side. The researchers are covered head to toe in white cloth. Unrelatedly, they are sexless. They don't draw lakes in forests. They don't play classic guitar.

The endless sound of plastic curses mankind: through endless observation, experimentation, and verification, this hypothesis is becoming as scientifically sound as the flight formation of migrating birds. All existing types of truth have the same status. Researchers, who are pursuers of truth, dream of egalitarianism.

Truth goes beyond consent and nonconsent, tolerance and distrust. The researchers prefer facts over truth and falsehood. As a matter of fact, facts have no feelings. Facts don't require consolation.

What the researchers are fond of isn't a picture but a photo. This photo—which required over two hundred million altitude measurements, which is a combination and synthesis of over a thousand photos, which shows the entirety of the surface of Mars—illustrates what form of love the researchers are pursuing.

The collection of facts isn't a matter of taste. The researchers want a revolution.

PART 3

THE LUSH FOREST OF N'S
OUTDOOR WRITING CONTEST

I go to the writing contest with the fat-cheeked poet who wears his water bottle strapped diagonally across his chest. This short, fat-cheeked poet gets a prize in everything he participates in. When the essay starts, he goes off somewhere. I follow the poet. It's a lush forest. He's sitting there with his back against a tree. Maybe having his back against one tree is his special trick. His face deep in some book he's ruffling through. It's a dictionary. He finds a word he doesn't know and uses it in a poem, and with that poem he wins the prize. I steal his dictionary and run like hell. As I run, I speed-read the dictionary. When I turn around, the poet is sweating with his face buried deep in his papers. *Sseuksseuksseukseuk* is the sound of a poem being written. A word I don't know catches my eye.

House (verb): N arrives at home and opens the front door but there is no N. This is because N is somewhere else at that time. N thinks over each and every place they visited, closes all the doors. Leaves the house. *The fish market, butcher's, hat store, let's visit them all again, in order.* While walking N turns around for no reason. A house is like a beached sea lion on its back, a chubby one that looks like it could sweat even in death. N looks at the ground. Walks. Bangs head-first into someone's sturdy chest. Oops! Lifts their head and looks up. It's not N. Because they're taller than N. N walks. There's no reason to look back, but N keeps looking back. There's a house. The house remains a house. Walk. Turn around. No house. N has come far enough that it's out of sight. N returns to the house. Now that N is going toward the house, there is no house when N looks back. N tries thinking that the house is dead. Thinks of the word death. Death is just something that's thickly built up. N walks on.

N arrives at home and opens the front door but there is no N. This is because N is somewhere else. N sticks their face inside the dark interior of the house and looks around. Still not here . . . If there's no N, there's no need to go in, so N decides to sleep outside.

*

I go to a lush forest. I tear up the poem that used the unknown word. Come out of the lush forest now! The fat poet is sweating. I chuck the dictionary. Whack! The spine of the book strikes the poet and the poet falls backwards. They bounce back like a self-righting doll and sweat. It suddenly occurs to me that I have never seen a poet participate in a writing contest. The only poets who attend writing contests are you and me! To become the only poet to attend writing contests, I shove the poet with my two arms. I bundle the fat-cheeked poet in plastic wrap. Roll him away. Push him off a cliff. I enter the lush forest. I brush off the dictionary and sit in the place the poet was sitting. The place where the poet who went to writing contests was sitting is also a place where a human sat, so it's still warm. I start there, where the heat hasn't dissipated. I put my back against one tree. I bury my face in my papers and sweat. It's a quiet forest. *Sshiksshiksshiksshik* isn't a sound that the lush forest makes.

WHAT THE HALLWAY PREPARED

There's a hallway and
Window 1 and Window 2 face each other.

There is something Window 1 hasn't said. Window 2, by completing
    the not-saying of what Window 1 hasn't said,
prevents the hallway from disappearing.

The hallway's windows are always open eyes.
An open eye looks at an open eye.

I want to make you mad.

Window 1 passes through Window 2.
Window 1 looks at Window 2's forest. The cliff in the forest. The
white palm of the hand on the cliff. And the person smearing their
white palm everywhere, falling.

Someone staying up all night with open eyes looks at the eggplant-
colored ceiling. A person lives above them, supine, asleep. This person
stares with open eyes at the eggplant-colored person living above them.

Two people who died, eyes open.
Two lovers who parted, eyes open.
One person falling, eyes open.
To the dry hallway flies a dry bird.

Window 1 and Window 2 don't advance toward each other.
The hallway sustains the distance between them.

Window 1 and Window 2 love each other.
They are not close.

A REAL CARROT CRYING REAL TEARS

1. Someone goes to a carrot store to get carrots.
2. There isn't a single carrot that is truly carroty.
3. Where should they go?
4. Someone, believing that the past can be erased,
1. goes to the carrot store to get carrots.
5. Angels break into the store.
6. It rains.
7. The angels take out their umbrellas.
8. The carrots cry real tears,
9. Do you think you can wipe away a trickling past with a hanky?
10. But someone
1. goes to the carrot store to get carrots.
11. Winged angels are sitting around next to a stack of logs doing
   nothing. *Make sure to get enough sleep,* one of them says in a low
   voice.
12. The rest play with their umbrellas.
13. They sing

14.

We fold the world instead of an umbrella
We like that, so we
keep folding, folding.

15. The angels are in the grocery store forgiving people.
16. The carrots cry.

17. There are some carrots who don't cry.

18. Falling from the sky

19. going to get carrots

0. I don't count how many heavens there are.

LAWS OF MATH

$^{\circ}$ a

a needed a way to go back to itself

$a \div b \times b = a$
$a \times {}^{1}/_{b} \times b = a$

ex)
What is a human:
Divide human by misfortune and then multiply by misfortune to
   return to human

Is the world okay:
When the world was divided by meaningless weather and then
   multiplied by meaningless weather, the world wiggled its toes

You:
When you shoot the gun I put in your left hand you return to you

$^{\circ}$ The hunger of that hypotenuse

When the opponent knows the lengths of the two sides at a
   right angle, how very scared the hypotenuse is

$^{\circ}$ $a^2 + b^2 = c^2$

a with a clip in its hair runs
Holding its hand
b with a clip in its hair runs
Left with no choice,
c with a clip in its hair runs away

$$c = \sqrt{a^2 + b2}$$

c returns holding a saw
It rains hard and fast
a with a clip in its hair and
b with a clip in its hair
are hiding under the wet orchard's wet pagoda
and shivering
We haven't done anything wrong
c cuts off the roof and
puts the roof in
a potato sack,
ties it tight and
flings it off a cliff
Jumping *c* is stuffed and that taxidermy looks like this: jumping *a* and
jumping *b* holding hands in the rain

° When I woke up in the morning there were three arms so
one was alienated

° I saw a sweating whale in the sky

°

☆ runs toward me, a flapping sheet of paper in hand
and pastes
this paper on my forehead
which has a diary entry
written on it
(this was probably an act of suicide)

☆ is a bird that almost leaps to its death
(I'm upset by a world in which a bird that flew
into a window and died looks real—
that's what the diary said)

Am I okay? Am I hurt anywhere?

When I look down from the roof the pale
sheet of paper is frothing at the mouth
It dies without a scratch

° The once-dead notations gurgle and bubble

THE END

Pronounce *The End*
and your mouth shapes a natural smile
So when you're teaching a child who doesn't know how to smile
to smile
it's good to have them pronounce *The End*

Now, try saying *The End*
Pull back the ends of your lips on each side
the way you tug each end of a laundry line
the way you hang a white sheet over that line

We cut life's edges with scissors
on the stair landing

and we don't even know what the end looks like but
we stand like the end

When can you say *The End* and make it sound the prettiest?
Maybe that's the kind of thing we're thinking:
If we all
said *The End*
instead of *Cheese*
the moment the photo is taken
the world would be a bit brighter
Is this the thought we had?

You just have to laugh, you have many ends in you
at that place where the end and the end stand
at that angle of your neck when it's tilted back to shake down the pills

FIGHT AT THE PARK

It was at a park.
Gemelle and Strains gave Antoine the slip and headed to a motel.
Strains strips Gemelle.
Gemelle is an empty birdcage under her clothes.
The kind that comes easily to mind.
The kind with a rounded top
that looks more natural when the paint is chipped
and squeaks even when it is still.
Strains can't laugh. She has never slept
with a birdcage before especially
a birdcage without a bird . . .
The feeder in the birdcage is a tired purple.
Just do it!
Gemelle opens her eyes wide. Because there is no reply the poet
writes only up to this point, but
because hopeless situations are overcome by hopeless situations the
    poet
heads to the park where Antoine and the pigeon were left.
The pigeon stands
on one leg.
Actually, the pigeon has two legs.
One leg is hidden against its stomach.
It's just pretending to be injured today, as always. Antoine
sprints toward the pigeon and
the pigeon falls over. Instinctively

it stands back up on two legs. The pigeon
sighs and
folds a leg under its belly to hide it.
Antoine is, of course, hurt.
Why won't it pretend to be struggling in front of me?

While Antoine and the pigeon fight
it's summer.
People are incapacitated in the daytime. Gemelle
runs out of the hotel and heads to the park's evangelist.

It's the kind of summer when 2 o'clock in the afternoon twists its
body to be tardy at 2:01. The fat fly near the empty birdcage is also
at the park. It flies around with a wry smile wherever it goes.

The purslane weed standing next to the bench.
Someone's loneliness must be
supplemented by
someone else's loneliness so
you'd think there would be a purslane
standing next to that purslane but
that isn't always the case.
Why do these things happen?
The evangelist
on the bench doesn't answer
just hands over
a chocolate bar that's become recklessly sweet,

saying, *The labor shortage*
in heaven means angels
sometimes have to fill in for the devil
but that shouldn't ruin anyone's warm summer day.

(___)
::::::
abc

His *two gapped front teeth probably make his entire person sloppy, b* said of the 2nd floor man they'd never seen. *Because of the gap between his teeth he must have a body that lets a lot of wind through. c* looks up at the ceiling. Open palms, the dust that falls on them. From the floor above, the sound of a chair being dragged.

Why does that person walk like that, mom? *b* and *c* sit in a rocking chair and don't ask this to *a*, who thinks rocking thoughts. Every time the man walks around dragging his chair, dust falls from between the long panels in the ceiling.

a and *b* and *c* sleep squished together like *abc*. They oppose each other's desire for sleep. The first one to jump into dreamland doesn't shout *Jump!* If you sleep with your mouth open, dust falls in your dreams too.

a and *b* and *c* survived on the falling dust. *a* sits on the rocking chair and quietly rocks. *a* reads the newspaper to become irrelevant to themselves. Even under the apricot tree in the yard, dust falls on *b* and *c*.

You're humming again!
Are you anxious again?

b looks
at the shadows
torn up and falling
piling
on *c*.

The apricot tree repeated its fruit. Tree shadow, the definite ants unable
to feel a definite sorrow take the season away with them.

That man lives on the floor above us. We're not on the same level,
b coughs.
c dusts off the dust that lives on *b*'s head.
We can't meet with someone who's not on the same level as us.
The foreshadowing dust.
Mom, the second floor is quiet.
b
Mom, the second floor is quiet.
c

When they return home the table's left corner had moved a
   little.
The shoes at the front door are as before.

The skull hit the table and
someone ran out without putting their shoes on.
That's an easy thought.

a sits on the rocking chair, rocking back and forth, not reading the
same newspaper.

NAIL

It's nearly a sweet potato. No arms no legs the whole body is a bruise. Put a bruise on top of the bruise of a sweet potato whose whole body is covered with bruises, it doesn't show up. It's sitting on the bed. No arms no legs, the forehead is wide. There's a wound in the middle of its face the size of an unlaced sneaker. The wound is caved in, the depth of a sneaker's rubber sole. It has no arms, no legs, and its hair is long. The few strands of hair that come down over the forehead stick onto the wet wound that won't heal up. If the wound scabs over while the hairs are stuck, they'll never come out. *Germs are very small and shrewd.* The thing doesn't have a mouth, so this is something someone else has said or it's something the wound babbles. Light up the area around the wound with a candle the way you would light up a corner of a dark house to climb the wood stairs. The wound is still like subway station lockers at dawn. In the midst of its stillness it randomly spews blood. Silence hides some spasmodic part of itself, so you mustn't provoke it. The fresh spewed-out blood runs over the outline of the wound. It flows all over unable to find a direction. Hair is black even when soaked in blood. *The blood has crossed the line; it's a very dirty wound.* These words don't need to be said to be heard. The wound is only as deep as a hand's thickness. It glows with the sky's light. Like an elderly mushroom hidden in a lush forest, it's white and still. Light a candle to illuminate the wound. Hair floats onto the blood-damp forehead. Time flows. That means the hair that isn't ready to fall out will soon change into hair that is ready to fall out. Hair is dead to begin with. So dead that the bacteria that breaks down bodies has no interest in it. The dead-to-begin-with hair comes down onto the wound and they become one body. It's a wound with a clear outline. Because of its outline the pain it can feel is limited. Light a candle to illuminate the wound. According to the size of the wound there are constraints on the amount of pain that can be felt. Blood flows. Draw all the blood in the body to make an eight-centimeter nail, just long enough to hang the hat the thing often wore back when it used to walk.

WHEN YOU'RE SAD BRING A PIG'S ASS

Look at the pig's ass. It's a light pink. It's roundish and abundant. The pig's ass belongs to a different world than the colorful macarons on display sitting neat in a row in their sharp-edged box. The pig's ass doesn't dream. The pig's ass doesn't have a whole lot of choices. And if your mom keeps appearing? If she's all crumpled up, hanging onto a doorknob, and crying? Then summon a pig's ass. The shiny pig's ass that sweats so much isn't apologetic, not to anyone, nor does it compliment those who are long-suffering. Two in the morning. A comic book store. The fatty father in the childish shorts who has run away from home sits in a plastic chair too small for his body. He slurps instant ramen. The protagonist in the comic book has big eyes, and on the sea, the sun rises daily, there being no other choice. The protagonist is wearing an aimless straw hat, and there's a parrot on their shoulder. This protagonist who sweats even when the breeze blows has no friends but pretends to have many friends, and that is the eternal subject of this comic. The pig's ass never gives anyone its opinion. It doesn't ask you about your childhood. The pig's ass can't cry sob-sob-sob and because it has no pride it can't be rained on.

Then what about the pig's tail?
As if kindly refusing something
as if hiding its messed-up mind
as if the water in the toilet is imperceptibly swelling
the lost
pig's tail

is on alert
even when the huge pig sleeps deep-deep and sweating
its whole body
curly
curly
curly
curling.

AXE WIELDING CRAZY ASSED PERSON

that's an axe wielding crazy assed person that person asks me for
a pencil

a pencil I don't have a pencil that person draws in the sandpit
a house

draws
a house

with a door is possible
that person

opens the door in the house in the drawing and walks through
    whether or not to leave through the backdoor
that

isn't something this person is hesitating about when it doesn't open
    even after the doorknob is broken
kicking

and pushing with their ass and finally breaking it open with an axe
that kind of thought

doesn't occur to this person
this person

is an ass wielding crazy axed person who is this person I
didn't

cry this person swung the axe, don't you have any self-respect,
they

shout
night

it was night a cold breeze blew behind my back an utterly
clueless

clueless breeze who is it this person couldn't take their real
axe

and come out of their home this person is a person with an axe
stuck

in his ass
this person

cries people need to cry more often thinks the person with the axe

when someone cries
truly

they become anti-establishment so you come here,

this
isn't something the person says the person
waits

for the waves they
believe

it's possible to wait for the waves this person and the ass and the axe
together

are not insane
no

that's not the reason this person knows the truth
the bird

hits the window and dies over and over again god isn't so skilled
you

see, that kind of thought was possible even when the axe was laid
down

what did you do just now? the axe doesn't ask god dead
bird

included it was a house we should repaint it, I say
no

bad words I am a nice person in the house made of ass and axe
a person

lives here axe wielding ass crazy a real person lived
once

I was curious the waves came and swept clean the sandpit why
    did this person
draw

their house
in so. much.

great detail?

LIFE CENTERED AROUND

I think with you at the center of my thoughts. Europa orbits Jupiter and centers Jupiter in its thoughts. Europa thinks about its day, spinning around that thing that is slowest to come when you want to escape. It massages its swollen feet, points its toes to the wall, points them back. It spun through the day while deferring the day. It spins with no intention to arrive, no intention to push away. Spinning shallowly it thinks of shallow outer space. Europa wets its ankles and is in pain. The pain orbits around Jupiter. Europa hurts. It spins until it forgets Jupiter and thinks of the moment it spun around someone who wasn't there. It's space and space smiles like a doll whose neck is the only part that turns. When Europa thinks of space it thinks of the year 5000 or just before the year 5000 or just after the year 5000. It thinks of a star orbiting a faraway star. It writes down a date it can't live in and writes a diary entry where the letters orbit around letters. The spinning makes them round. The left side of the doll's face is spinning to arrive at its right side. It smiles from ear to ear as its neck becomes bright blue. A letter came from far away. A letter without an orbit. Every letter in it is a round fence. A bug smoothly steps over the back of another bug. Pushing forward a little at a time. It erects the walls it has passed behind it and spins. It presses its back against the thing it left behind. It goes forward.

HE'S NOT CRAZY YET
—TO THE FOG

1

A fog like a bus stop descended in a village with no fog.
The people missed the fog for a long time.
He puts the fog on like an old undershirt and unburdens himself of
    shame.
He records a single layer of fog.

2

The girls look out the window at the lunula-colored fog. It's said that
the fog won't be erased even if the windows are rubbed. And that's
how they came to love the fog.

3

It's comforting how you aren't shown the things that are far away
ahead of time, said the janitor, brushing away the palm lines people left
behind. No one would be sad if an elephant appeared in the fog like an
island. Since far away things can't be seen in the first place, anyone in
the fog must get used to suspicions.

4

It feels like soaking in an empty bathtub with your kneecaps rounded. Even if someone who thought this drowned in the fog, no one would mourn them, so the world went on quietly.

5

Now now, look at me, if you want to steal the fog, shhhh . . . be quiet . . . you just have to fold up the fog like this, like this, and stack them here . . . shhh . . . said an old woman as rough and dry as a head of garlic, as she touched the closet's doorknob. She's crazy but not crazy. She's just figured out how to shift a bit of the past onto the fog.

6

No words are exchanged. Everyone endures the fog by waiting for their past, but they don't realize the worn hem of their pants is shedding one thread after the other. Everyone quiets their footsteps.

7

The children in the fog put down their own chimneys and even out their breaths. They take care so their feet don't fall into someone else's chimney. The children lift their heels and run lightly.

8

When you left I wailed at the top of my lungs. When I cry only the shadows get soaked. When a pop song for locating a lost person rings out from inside the fog, the people finally set out to look for missing chimneys, dropped fingernails, etc. That's just everyone's secret life. It has nothing to do with the palms that can't be read clearly because their underlines have been erased.

9

In the fog a man with a nose like a bookmark sells lottery tickets. The reason people play the lottery isn't to hit the jackpot. It's to shake off any lingering what-ifs. In that way, the lottery and the fog are alike. The man hands out lottery tickets in the fog, and people scrape off the silver ink with rusted coins.

10

At the frayed edge of the fog, a pierrot dressed up as a pierrot wets the fog with a stiff stream of piss. Someone gets down low on the ground to avoid the pee. The soles of the fog's feet are chilly.

PART 4

POEM WRITTEN WITH A MOSQUITO

The young poets Antoine, Gemelle, and Strains went to a poet's
lecture.
The topic of the lecture was shattering this way and that way.

The poet on the podium was shattering this way and that way.

The mosquitoes came for them. It was summer. Summer of
floating clouds that have never been ironed.

Seated in the very back row, Antoine, Gemelle, and Strains followed
the lecturer and took out things from their bags that could shatter
this way and that way.

From her bag Antoine took out the woman she met yesterday. The
woman smoked cigarettes in every situation. It gave the impression
that she was a consistent and diligent person. They emerged from
the bar and parted in the rain.
Goodbye
Farewell
Fare even better

Strains opened her bag. Mom tried to come out so she pushed her
back in.
Because she said she loved her yesterday but she didn't say that the day
before.

Gemelle couldn't open her bag, the knot was too complicated.

Everyone can become an artist!
The lecturer showed them a photo of baby turtles. On the beach
the baby turtles were birthed haphazardly.
A mosquito
stuck itself to Antoine's left shin.
How pitiful, the mouth that stabs and sucks.

Mosquito!

Strains smacked Antoine's left shin
with her stick. The mosquito
saddened slyly and
moved away.

The poet on the podium kept on shattering this way and that way.
The newborn baby turtles looked old.
It'd be fine to quit living,
thought someone who was not the mosquito.

The mosquito had nothing to do. All it wanted was to also meddle
        in someone's sadness. According to plan

the mosquito sat and stabbed its mouth into Gemelle's upper arm.
        The blood got sucked out and the bag's knot loosened. The mini-
        poets

Strains, Gemelle, and Antoine came out of Gemelle's bag.

Mini Gemelle Why is childbirth so uniquely difficult for humans?
Mini Antoine There's not much space between the legs. And babies
    have ultra-large heads.
Mini Strains Human heads are becoming bigger and bigger.
Mini Antoine That's what you call evolution.
Mini Strains Eventually their heads will be too big, and humans won't
    be able to come out of their mother's wombs. A day will come when
    people will live in their mothers' wombs.
Mini Antoine That's what you call evolution.

Gemelle grabbed the mini-poets and shoved them in her bag and
    made a more complicated knot.
Antoine slapped the mosquito on Gemelle's upper arm. Instantly,
    lights out. No one saw the mosquito's guts.

A genteel flight to Strains's nape. There, a mosquito caught its breath.

The turtles whose birth made them awkward
were scuttling somewhere.
Shatter this way shatter that way.
Become born!
Everyone can become an art . . .
Run away!
Run away!
Run away!

The poets Strains, Antoine, and Gemelle ran out of the lecture with
the mosquito.
Behind the young poets who had come outside
a single, never-been-ironed cloud floated by.
It was a warm and windless day.

THE BOOK FROM FAR AWAY

When the book is opened, the sentences are immersed in creating double knots. They twist their bodies constantly. Like little bugs under a rock, they repeat pointless motions for years. The sentences burn black at the edges because they focus only on themselves. They pay no attention to their environment, they cannot look toward the future, they only stay in one place and dig a groove, no matter what, to make a mark on the floor. For this they twist their bodies as much as they can and repeat the deepening motion.

The child worries that the child who has brought this book to them has come from too far away. The child doesn't need this kind of book. The child needs a book that can be read. The kind of book that will allow them to shout, *I read this kind of book!* A book from too far away isn't needed in the world.

The child who has come from far away pokes one of the sentences with their white finger—the sentence that looks like all the rest, the sentence that twists its body to the same degree. *I like this sentence, what about you?* they ask. *Yeah, this sentence seems to have made lonely knots for longer than the other sentences, and the way it twists its body is unique,* says the other child, pretending to agree.

By the window reflecting the sunset, the child and the child from far away pore over the book. Meanwhile the sunset has dyed red the gray lines of the twisted bugs. The two children clasp their knees together and look into the book. The child suddenly comes to their senses. They chuck the child from far away and the book out the window.

The child locks the front door. The child needs more things to lock, so they imagine a few doors in their mind. They lock the doors one at a time. On an island where no one lives, in the shade of a tree that nobody knows, a pointless rock is breathing, and the rock nurtures bugs whose legs change numbers every time they're counted. To forget this, the child locks more doors. In a little crack in the skull, on top of a precarious rock, a bug reveals itself.

FROTTAGE

Dali's life can be summarized as follows:

> 1904 *Attempted Birth*
> 1921 *Attempted Birth*
> 1947 *Attempted Birth*
> 1952 *Attempted Birth*
> 1977 *Attempted Birth*
> 1989 *Death*

Dali grips a green twist-up crayon.
Within his casket, he writes his last sentences on the inside of the
casket's lid.

Written near his big toe:

> *The way paper can be folded into a paper crane,*
> *shadow is folded into a crane.*
> *The way paper can be folded into a paper crane,*
> *objects are folded into metaphor.*

Near his skull:

Surrealism is impossible and
the only thing that's possible
is reality incapacitating reality.

If a casket lid, once shut, is re-opened,
people would lose their trust in the world.

CHILDREN GATHERED AT A PLACE THAT ISN'T AN EXIT

Child G died.

Child A sent a text to Child B, C, D, E, and F.

Come to exit 4.

Child A waited for her friends at exit 3, thinking it was exit 4.

Child B, holding flowers,
went out through exit 3,
thinking there was no way Child A got the exit right.

Child C, a child with two eyes,
went to exit 3
because Child A said to come to exit 4.

Child D, who was the shape of an equilateral triangle, met a
    fly in the subway.

Lead by the bitter laughter of the fly
that seemed to say
You think death is big and meaty?
Child D went to exit 3.

Child E, a questionable character,
went to exit 3 because she felt it was right.

Child F with a big head
believed that all things labelled "exit" were lies so he exited wherever
and wherever turned out to be exit 3.

The real exit was exit 3 and

Child A, Child B, Child C, Child D, Child E, and Child F
joined hands, side by side.
They went to dead Child G.

HISTORY AND WAR

The Earth can't believe in space.

To see space, I'd have to be bigger than space
or far away from space, so
how am I supposed to believe in you?

The graffiti that X saw in the bathroom says:

Why do you get stuck in an elevator once a month? Why is it always you that
gets stuck?

From Space's perspective, Earth
is a lost Rubik's Cube,
unsolved and
rolling around under the bed and

Earth rolls,
diligently,
diligently,
it revolves
its body,

constantly having to be supplied its own reality.

BREAD

The poet and the novelist order one Merry Strawberry Cream Smoothie.
A small crocodile with no eyes, nose, or mouth—the tail a little frayed—
hangs from the novelist's backpack. She takes out the novel she finished
yesterday. The poet reads the novels the novelist gives her as though
they were letters.

The poet has something to give to the novelist too.
The famous writer A's book she read yesterday,
a short story collection, *Bread*.

Everything the poet wants to say A has said already, so when the poet
wants to know what she's thinking, she opens *Bread* and reads it, and
when she wants to forget what she's thinking, she chucks *Bread* under
the bed.

Bread is a story about Bread.

Starting with
The bread I was going to eat tomorrow morning . . .
and ending with
The bread I was going to eat tomorrow morning . . .

The poet hands the novelist *Bread* and
hopes that the novelist will notice
that part of her life

where instead of
"Love me"
she began to say
"I have a cold"
or
"I want to go!"
or
"Could you water the plants please?"

But
The novel that the novelist hands to the poet is also titled *Bread*.
Bread has become a hot topic in Korean literature because of the famous
writer A's success. To write an excellent novel, to make good bread, the
novelist shaved her whole body. The moment she sees the novel's title,
the poet's heart is refracted like a hand put into a bucket of water.

While the poet reads the novelist's *Bread*, the novelist
stares at the whipping cream of the Merry Strawberry Cream
Smoothie, oversized compared to the cup.
Ridiculous.
This is the novelist's true feeling.

While untrustworthy strawberry pieces sit on the whipped cream

as if cascading
the poet reads *Bread* and—
The novelist's *Bread* is similar to A's *Bread*.

That is to say
the story's structure is similar,
the way it ends with the child who goes to get bread for tomorrow
going out tomorrow to get bread for the next day,
and how in between
it's dark like a tunnel
filled with
the stories of identical bread doughs
going through
a long oven
one after the other,

a story that is a boring list of doughs that are good because they have·
no eyes, nose, or mouth.

The novelist wanted to write an excellent story, didn't she?
After all, she shaved all the hair on her body
and then wore a long-sleeved shirt and long pants
to this meeting with the poet in the middle of summer
to hide it.
The line the poet underlined last night while reading *Bread* goes like
this:

Bread doesn't go sour so easily. As long as you don't leave it lonely for a long
time, bread doesn't sour and, no matter where you tear it, bread shows a plain
and expressionless surface.

Her heart is in her heart and in *Bread* and in *Bread* too. Wherever you
tear it, it's still the same heart.
Novels,
stories,
one is enough.
This is something the poet thinks unconsciously though she doesn't
    mean it
and doesn't say it out loud.
An afternoon
threatened by the impending collapse of the cream on the Merry
    Strawberry Cream Smoothie, between her and her.

They felt a shared feeling when they ordered something that would
    collapse, but when she feels that the half of the strawberry
    embedded in the cloud-like whipped cream looks perfect for
    foreshadowing the fact that they need consolation she feels it
    alone.

PIMPLE POPPING

I pop a pimple. The pimple appeared at the border between my left nostril and cheek. I was going to go on a picnic to the Arario Sculpture Park with darling you. We'd promised to eat grapes under the park's zelkova tree. But now this pimple, with its uncomfortable body near my nose. The white dot swollen in the middle sits there precariously like a pagoda in the middle of an artificial pond. It's easy to make someone cry. *Are you crying?* Go up to anyone, put your small hand on their shoulder and look into their face. I take out a rusted needle. I heat up the needle tip in the stove's blue flame for 2 - 3 seconds. Pop, I burst the white dot. The white dot opens its thin eye. Mystery fluid comes weeping out of the hole. I take a tissue and wipe the tears the hole is crying. I bring my face right up to the mirror. I squeeze the inflamed area with the tips of my two index fingers. I squeeze the way you squeeze a used-up toothpaste tube by rolling it up. No more liquid comes out. *Are you done crying?* Ask this to someone who you think has no more tears left to cry, and from the hole, an unexpected liquid will explode out to a low height and subside. Sticky, half-opaque beige liquid. It reminds me that I haven't seen blood yet. When you cry, you should cry until you see a little blood. Because when it comes to blood, everyone has a stubborn streak. Because the blood comes at the end. Because, like the roots of a tree, it grips the soil until the moment it's uprooted. A boat. Small fishing boat. You're dozing off. The pulley that was slowly spinning, seated at the corner of the boat, speeds up. Your chin is perched on the string of your wide hat. The sea breeze dries the black liquid that runs down your chin. *Thunk,* the rope spins to the end and catches. The hat, caught on the side of the boat, flutters in the sea breeze. You see blood. Take another tissue. Wipe. Blood is clear. Blood is soft. Blood is stupid. Blood grips. It knows this is the end.

APARTMENT

There was a gurgle from the stomach of one out of ten thousand.

There was a gurgle from the stomach of one out of a thousand.

There was a gurgle from the stomach of one out of a hundred.

There was a gurgle from the stomach of one out of ten.

There was a gurgle from the stomach of one out of one.

Dish: broken.

A large mountain: in sight.

She jumped from the 22nd floor.

SILENCE ON A TABLE

At an angular table, <a tragic event> is gripping a fork and knife in each hand and having a stare-down with <a tragic event that hasn't happened yet> sitting on the other side of the table.

A tragic event: I'm a person too.

A tragic event that hasn't happened yet: I'm a person too.

—Oh!—

The excellent artwork knew the tragic event that hasn't happened yet. It kept the knowledge to itself. It didn't share it with anyone.

THE POET AND THE PIG

The pig is dying. Because the poet is raising a pig, they write pig-poems. The poet lays down hay for the pig and washes the pig and sleeps with the pig. The pig is nearing death so it cries sometimes in the kitchen and goes out at night and comes back at night. Even if the pig doesn't cry its body is swollen fat, and because its body is big it dreams big difficult dreams.

It's the pig's last hour. The poet never made a friend, has only lived with the pig. The poet feels pig-sized feelings and writes pig-sized poems. A *pig is a little too big to be considered a poem*, the poet fails to think.

The pig is dying. The pig and the poet go to the riverbank. The poet doesn't know the pig's death. But the poet knows that death is similar for everyone. *Like a zipper on the back of a dress, something you can't reach yourself but is easy for someone else to zip*, writes the poet. The pig in need of help looks up at the poet.

Help me.
The pig asks for the zipper to be pulled down because the pig
    can't breathe. The poet looks at the pig and writes
Pigs have swollen bodies from birth to death
in the poem.

The pig is dying. *Swollen things seem like they endure everything*, the poet thinks. The pig sweats. Dusk falls on the riverbank where they sit and play the game they always play.

The poet throws a rock and the pig watches.
Concentric rings appear on the surface of the water.
In the ring a smaller concentric ring
and inside the smaller concentric ring an even smaller concentric ring.
Concentric rings appear one after another,
small, and therefore good for belonging somewhere.
The pig and poet watch the rings get smaller and smaller.
The poet doesn't write,
If you keep getting smaller and smaller you can safely disappear.

Nothing by the riverbank is bigger than the pig. The dying pig
looks at the small things. The small rock and small birds and
the small dew that can belong to the blade of grass because
it's smaller than the blade of grass and the bugs that curl their
bodies. The pig is dying. A mosquito lands on the pig's back.

The poet writes
A mosquito dies a death the size of a mosquito and a pig dies a death the size of
a pig, so a pig dies more than a mosquito
in the poem.

The pig is dying. Because the poet has no friends, they write only about
the pig. The pig dies soon. Time goes on. The poet and the pig think
time is like clasped hands resting on a knee: indifferent toward everyone.

The poet looks at the pig. The poet looks at the short and cheerful tail on its honest ass and cries. Instead of saying, *I am sad*, the dying pig sets its six nipples down on the ground and collapses. *The grass pinned under the pig's belly must be warm.* The poet can write that kind of thing in a poem. The pig can't feel the whole sadness of dying, but it feels a part of that sadness and closes its eyes. The pig dies and the poet writes. The poet only writes about bodies that don't diminish, even after they're dead.

IDENTITY

I take any book at random. The library is quiet and brightly lit. The librarian wears a heaven-colored button down every day and guards the counter. Because the librarian always wears the same colored button down, it's impossible to distinguish today from yesterday, yesterday from the day before, yesterday from the day after tomorrow.

I pick up another book. It's about a dead father sitting on a rock at the corner of a sculpture park and eating convenience store soup. He eats the soup with a not-so-sturdy clear plastic spoon. He dribbles some soup on the rock. The story ends. I open another story. The rock dribbles the rest of the soup.

Because I need a mental diet, I read books daily. I read until the content of every book becomes the same. Because the librarian wears the same clothes, it's impossible to distinguish between the sad story I read yesterday and the unhappy story I read today.

A man reads with his back to me while I read with my back to him. We sigh competitively. We sigh, telling each other that your sighing is ruining the precious silence of the library. You're ruining it. No, you're ruining it. Is he reading the story of the rock who cries soup-tears with soup that someone else spilled because he's tearless too? Listen up, but no, isn't it the child in me who sighs and not me?

The child whose only possession is a bruise-colored rubber balloon has nothing else to do. So the child blows up the balloon. The child blows until the balloon is about to burst and then, slowly, the child lets the air out. I take in that air and sigh. If the balloon bursts the child will have nothing to play with. Because yesterday-me and today-me are indistinguishable, the balloon maintains its bruise color.

We read the book where a rock cries instead of a person and maintain our identical identities. We know that if the balloon bursts, there will be no more need to hold our breaths, to take revenge by breathing, to read books where people are dying.

The man slams his book shut. Just now, someone gave up on me.

IS THE FORK AN APPROPRIATE IMPLEMENT WITH WHICH TO STAB A CHERRY TOMATO?

A child goes to a French restaurant with a child. The child sitting across from the child has large eyes with clear whites. The legs of the table are covered with a long tablecloth. The child's legs don't reach the floor. The child decides the places his feet can't touch are the ocean. On the flat porcelain dish are many just-washed cherry tomatoes. The child on the other side begins to drop her fork.

The child looks at the child on the other side. Standing behind the child with clear eyes is an infinity of children with clear eyes. Like a paper doll that is ten paper dolls stacked on top of each other, like individual paper dolls that fan out into ten dolls holding hands when you unfold them. When the clear-eyed child drops her fork, behind her, the creepy clear-eyed children fluctuate like ocean waves. One of them bursts forward and snatches the fork before it falls to the ground.

When the fork falls, a child with nothing but whites for eyes hurls the napkins and candlestick into the air. The child behind her catches them like a bouquet. The out-of-formation child rescues the fork. She returns to formation, and folds one arm at a right angle, hanging a napkin over it. With her left hand she picks up the candlestick. A small flame flickers. The child wonders, *Is the fork an appropriate implement with which to stab a cherry tomato?*

A cherry tomato is very round, and because it's round, it's distinct, and distinct things make you want to stab them with a fork. From every direction, the possibility of sudden danger is the same. An ocean organism of an old model and a cherry tomato. A single-celled organism floating here and there with the currents of an old sea and a cherry tomato—what an old act it is to stab these things with a fork. Splattering in every direction—how stupid. The cherry tomato on the table looks around to the left, to the right. About this cherry tomato, looking equally toward every direction, every direction carrying equal risk of someone approaching—

A height that is too high to touch with your feet on the floor creates an ocean underneath those feet. The child on the other side drops her fork infinitely. In the world on the other side live solemn children who rescue cherry tomatoes and forks. If there is an "other side" no matter where you sit, if you become the "other side" to someone else no matter where you sit, I'll roll my body round and become red. The child stabs with a fork—an explosion in every direction.

THESE WOMEN

Antoine, Strains, and Gemelle read the following line in a book:

A person is composed of two parts:
The soul and the body

They thought.

Gemelle shouts,
A person is composed of an open birdcage and the bird that flew away

Strains stops walking.
A person is the composite of one stick and the fly beat up with that stick

Antoine raises her hand.
A person is made up of two parts:
Their finger and all the things that finger hasn't pointed to

They close the book and go home.
When will home return to its sanity?

In summer, a season stingy of sadness,
they don't ask that kind of question.

METHODS OF CHOOSING

A mushroom grows.
Can you believe it?
It stinks, memory.
Let's not write our diary entries in the bathroom.
Car headlights on a rainy day
transparent
slashes that won't go on for long.
A clothes hanger without clothes.
A pebble that won't eat.
A rolling
bald head.
Mushrooms grow
in groups at the stumps of dead and fallen trees
so why does the laccaria mushroom
a.k.a. the deceiver
try to end its life?
A human who isn't a mushroom expert had feelings for the
mushroom.
For some reason I feel like a mushroom
could easily explode.
The mushroom
and I
dream.
Two legs peddling wildly in reality.
The eyebrows

are

only visible from the side

because once love cools, it's profile-view

only.

Let's write

our diary on the toilet.

Let's draw pictures.

Sadness in the shape of a single cell.

Being disappointed in a cell.

Being disappointed on a rainy day by the scream of slashes that car
    headlights can't hear.

A clothes hanger that doesn't know how to wear clothes is

the underground world of mushrooms.

High-speed photography showed us hope.

The side of the mushroom that crumples.

Wearing a bamboo hat, the mushroom cried.

I want to sprout.

Will the asexual reproduction of humans be the salvation of humans?

If you flip over the mushroom's hat: sadness.

Even the asexual being

that writes diary entries

has a steady need for toilet paper.

The solitude of the pathogen stuck in the solitary room of the ear
    canal.

Why doesn't the mushroom have eyebrows?

Mountain-born

small fires, tread them out.

With a shovel, dig the ground and
bury a small water.
If you see
a face,
cover it with soft dirt.

PILLAR OF BOOKS

I go to the library. It's a wide rectangle from the outside, but inside it's a spire. The high walls have giant stained-glass windows. The too-large windows weaken the walls, and the windows indiscriminately accept everything that passes through. That's my thought, which the librarian Edmond Jabes says is wrong.

The thin chain attached to the left lens of Edmond's glasses hang down to his shoulders. I think, *This place has very high ceilings,* and Edmond answers, *That's because the books have to be stacked high.* He opens the lamp lid and fills it with oil and then lights the wick.

On the bookshelf there are only books. The books are stacked in pillars. Gnomes putter around them. The gnomes bend their waists and twist their necks horizontally to look at the titles. They look at the bottom of a pillar of books. The books you want to read are always at the bottom of the pillar. I think of the books I want to read and those books are at the bottom of a pillar of books.

The pillars of books are tilted toward something. I think of tilted buildings. People go wild over things that can't stand straight like the Tower of Pisa. The pillars of books are touching in the way that things that could fall over at any moment are touching. Things that lean are biased towards something. I think of the human body that is straight on the outside but tilted one way or another on the inside. The heart is tilted to the left, the liver to the right, so humans walk straight. I think, *Tilted buildings cultivate people who sleep tilted toward the wall,* and Edmond reads my thoughts and says them out loud for me.

He clears a path by pushing long texts sprawled around the floor aside with his staff. Sometimes he whacks the small bare heads of the gnomes with his staff. He says he hits them because they aren't focused on reading, but he only picks on the gnomes who sit with their backs against a pillar, deeply immersed in books.

The gnomes knock down a pillar of books to get the books they want. They build up the pillar again. The gnomes hit the books and spit at the books and swear at the books. Understandably so, I think. Books are rude. Books steal your love and make people tilt this way or that way. They stare at only the wall and that weakens the wall. They make a window in the wall and force you to peek outside.

The gnomes topple a pillar to get to the books at the bottom. The books stack into a tower. They lean. Tilt. Spill. Get rebuilt. I think, *Reading a book at the bottom is the equivalent of reading all the books stacked above it. That one book sums up all the books above it,* and Edmond admonishes me, calls my thought complacent. A sunbeam sparkles on the handful of thin, winding hairs on the gnomes' heads. Light glances off their old thoughts. Edmond says, *You who thought the gnomes are exhausted, you haven't read enough.*

NOTES:

In "What Got Seen By The Two Ears the Passing Dog Ate," the fact about honeybees comes from the chapter titled "The Honey Bee's Hot Pot Tactic" in the book *The Whimsical Survival Strategies of Small Insects* by Yasutomi Kazuo.

In "Laws of Science," the statements about poems are based on the three characteristics of modern science defined in *Beyond UFOs* by Jeffrey Bennett.

Procrustes, in "Spare Parts," is a character in Greek and Roman mythology who killed people by stretching or chopping their limbs to fit a bed.

The photo in "White Factory" refers to a photo of Mars on page 9 of *Beyond UFOs* by Jeffrey Bennett.

ACKNOWLEDGEMENTS

Thank you to the magazines and journals that published poems from this book: *Puerto Del Sol, The Adroit Journal, Asymptote, Black Warrior Review, Columbia Journal, Copper Nickel,* and *Cordite Poetry Review.* A few poems were also published on Action Books' blog.

I submitted some of these translations to the Modern Korean Literature Translation Awards and was awarded the commendation prize in poetry. Thank you to the *Korea Times* for hosting the award and thank you to the judges. I used some of the prize money on stickers and pens from Korea, which was comforting to have because COVID-19 prevented me from visiting Korea over the summer.

Thank you to Jake Levine, who edited this manuscript. Thanks for caring so much about every poem, though perhaps it is not great for your health to care that much about every poem.

Thank you to Janaka Stucky and Carrie Adams at Black Ocean. Thank you to the typesetter Taylor Waring. Thank you to anyone else that I didn't personally interact with at Black Ocean who contributed to the publishing of this book.

All work necessitates great volumes of complaining. Thank you to Soeun Seo, who was my roommate for the majority of the time I was translating this book. It was satisfying to complain to them in detail, as they're a translator too.

Thanks to Jack Jung, who translated some of these poems right around the time I translated them and generously ceded the project of translating this book to me. Thanks also for your pep talks and for showing me the nice tweets about me.

Thanks to Moon Bo Young for writing these poems and being a joy to correspond with. Let's hang out soon.

AUTHOR

Moon Bo Young is a poet who has a hard time waiting for her nail polish to dry. She was born on Jeju Island, in 1992. She graduated Korea University with a degree in education. When it got windy on Jeju Island, she put a flat rock on top of her hat. She debuted as a writer in 2016. In 2017, she won the Kim Soo Young Prize for her book *Pillar of Books*, and with the prize money, she had a pizza party with her friends. To practice living daily life, she started a Youtube channel, "Some Poet's Vlog." She also publishes a one-person literary magazine called *A Bajillion Things Moon Bo Young*, and subscribers get her fiction, poetry, and journal entries in the mail. She likes pizza more than poems, and she likes journaling more than pizza, and she loves her friends more than journaling. She has two books of poetry, *Pillar of Books* and *Battle Ground*, and a book of essays, *The Many Ways to Hate People*.

TRANSLATOR

Hedgie Choi is a fellow at the Michener Center for Writers. She co-translated *Hysteria* by Kim Yi Deum. Her poems have appeared in *Washington Square Review*, *Beloit Poetry Journal*, *West Branch*, *The Journal*, and elsewhere.

ABOUT THE SERIES

Black Ocean :: Moon Country publishes new English translations of contemporary Korean poetry by both mid-career and up-and-coming poets who debuted after the IMF crisis. By introducing work that comes out of our shared milieu, this series not only aims to widen the field of contemporary Korean poetry available in English translation, but also to challenge orientalist, neo-colonial, and national literature discourses. Our hope is that readers will inhabit these books as bodies of experience rather than view them as objects of knowledge, that they will allow themselves to be altered by them, and emerge from the page with eyes that seem to see "a world that belongs to another star."*

*From the poem "Moon Country Mischief" by Kim Soo-young